THE MANAGER

by Darrin Shaughnessy

Winner of the
American College Theater Festival
Short Play Award

SAMUEL FRENCH, INC.

45 WEST 25TH STREET   NEW YORK 10010
7623 SUNSET BOULEVARD HOLLYWOOD 90046
LONDON   TORONTO

Copyright © 1994 by Darrin Shaughnessy

ALL RIGHTS RESERVED

CAUTION: *Professionals and amateurs are hereby warned that THE MANAGER is subject to a royalty. It is fully protected under the copyright laws of the United States of America, the British Commonwealth, including Canada, and all other countries of the Copyright Union. All rights, including professional, amateur, motion picture, recitation, lecturing, public reading, radio broadcasting, television, and the rights of translation into foreign languages are strictly reserved. In its present form the play is dedicated to the reading public only.*

The amateur live stage performance rights to THE MANAGER *are controlled exclusively by Samuel French, Inc., and royalty arrangements and licenses must be secured well in advance of presentation. PLEASE NOTE that amateur royalty fees are set upon application in accordance with your producing circumstances. When applying for a royalty quotation and license please give us the number of performances intended, dates of production, your seating capacity and admission fee. Royalties are payable one week before the opening performance of the play to Samuel French, Inc., at 45 W. 25th Street, New York, NY 10010-2751; or at 7623 Sunset Blvd., Hollywood, CA 90046-2795, or to Samuel French (Canada), Ltd., 80 Richmond Street East, Toronto, Ontario, Canada M5C 1P1.*

Royalty of the required amount must be paid whether the play is presented for charity or gain and whether or not admission is charged.

Stock royalty quoted on application to Samuel French, Inc.

For all other rights than those stipulated above, apply to Samuel French, Inc.

Particular emphasis is laid on the question of amateur or professional readings, permission and terms for which must be secured in writing from Samuel French, Inc.

Copying from this book in whole or in part is strictly forbidden by law, and the right of performance is not transferable.

Whenever the play is produced the following notice must appear on all programs, printing and advertising for the play: "Produced by special arrangement with Samuel French, Inc."

Due authorship credit must be given on all programs, printing and advertising for the play.

ISBN 0-573-69487-7

For Ina Louise Shaughnessy
and
Stephen W. Shaughnessy,
my mother and my father

No one shall commit or authorize any act or omission by which the copyright of, or the right to copyright, this play may be impaired.

No one shall make any changes in this play for the purpose of production.

Publication of this play does not imply availability for performance. Both amateurs and professionals considering a production are *strongly* advised in their own interests to apply to Samuel French, Inc., for written permission before starting rehearsals, advertising, or booking a theatre.

No part of this book may be reproduced, stored in a retrieval system, or transmitted in any form, by any means, now known or yet to be invented, including mechanical, electronic, photocopying, recording, videotaping, or otherwise, without the prior written permission of the publisher.

IMPORTANT BILLING AND CREDIT REQUIREMENTS

All producers of *The Manager must* give credit to the Author of the Play in all programs distributed in connection with performances of the Play and in all instances in which the title of the Play appears for purposes of advertising, publicizing or otherwise exploiting the Play and/or a production. The name of the Author *must* also appear on a separate line, on which no other name appears, immediately following the title, and *must* appear in size of type not less than fifty percent the size of the title type.

The Manager was originally staged as a workshop production with the American Southwest Theatre Company, Las Cruces, New Mexico with the following cast:

STEVE..............................Triney Sandoval
WOMAN.........................Kristin Middleton
SHELLY......................Susan Michele Nash
MANNY.............................Scott Anderson

Directed by :   Kim McCallum & Mark Medoff

The Manager was produced at the Arena Theatre in Fullerton, California, entered into the American College Theatre Festival and subsequently went on to the John F. Kennedy Center in Washington D.C. with the following cast:

STEVE...................................... Jim Gray
WOMAN.......................Samantha Hadfield
SHELLY.............................. Lisa Wilson
MANNY..............................Jeff Swarthout

Directed by: Tom Sundstrom & Dr. Joe Arnold
Scenery by: Lara Hanneman
Lighting by: Lisa Cindrich
Production Stage Manager: Nicole West

CHARACTERS

STEVE, early twenties
WOMAN, late twenties
SHELLY, early twenties
MANNY, early thirties

TIME & PLACE

The present.

An efficiency apartment in
Las Cruces, New Mexico

I would like to thank the following individuals, without whom this play might never have made it to print: Fawn R. Weaver, Tom Sundstrom, James J. Mangas, Mark Medoff, Kim McCallum, P. Jeff Sparks, Dean Hess, Joe Arnold and last but certainly most, Samantha Hadfield who gave her relentless support and encouragement.

THE MANAGER

SETTING: The play takes place in Steve's efficiency apartment in Las Cruces, New Mexico. The apartment consists of a living room, kitchenette, and bathroom (stage right) that is visible when the door is open. There is a bed in the living room with a large tapestry hanging over it. Set in one of the walls is a large gas heater. There is a door leading to the outside (stage left).

AT RISE: The LIGHTS come up on STEVE seated at the kitchen table writing intently. We should feel that he has been studying a long time. Suddenly HE stops. HE thinks. HE looks at the page in the typewriter. HE thinks some more. HE checks his notes to the side of the typewriter. HE finds something. Thinks.

STEVE. Yes! (*HE resumes typing intently.*) Yes, yes, yes, yes, yes. (*After a few moments the PHONE rings.*) No! (*HE continues typing. The PHONE rings again.*) No, no, no, no, no. (*The ringing continues as HE struggles to keep his train of thought.*) Leave me alone. (*More rings and HE has lost his concentration. HE answers the phone.*) Somebody better be dead! ... Oh, hi, baby ... Yeah, I'm still writing, or I was until the damn phone rang ... I did call ... 10:30 ... I know, look I was sitting here writing, I looked at the clock, it was 9:30, the next time I looked up it was 10:30 and so I called, you weren't there ... I didn't answer the phone because I'm trying to finish the damn thing ... It's coming along so I want to stay with it ... I miss you too ... Yes, I ate ... Some stuff ... I'm sure ... Yes I'm alone, whatta ya think; except for the midgets and the mules, but they don't count, right? ... Soon ... Come on, baby—don't ... You don't want to come over here, it's freezing ... No he didn't ... Please not tonight, don't do this ... Would you just ... Listen, there's this student, right, and he's got this assignment due on Monday morning, ... I'm not being condescending ... Alright, I don't mean to be and I'm not spazing out ... Okay, I am a little ... No, Shelly, you can't— ... okay, thanks ... I love you too, you know that? Ya. (*Hangs up the phone. Goes back to the typewriter.*) Christ!

(*Looks at the phone. Goes to typewriter and reads. Types a little, goes back to phone, picks it up, starts to dial, hangs up phone. Turns on some MUSIC. Gets himself a cup of coffee, goes back to typing. After a few moments HE is back on track, typing intently, when there is a KNOCK at the door; slight, almost inaudible. HE looks, decides it was nothing, continues writing. After a moment there is another KNOCK. This happens a couple of times, louder each time.*)

Finally HE gets up and turns down the MUSIC and opens the door.)

WOMAN. Oh, hi.

STEVE. Hi.

WOMAN. You're home; I was just outside. I thought maybe you were here so I knocked and then I figured you might not be here 'cuz you didn't answer. So ...

STEVE. Yeah, I wasn't sure if someone was knocking or not.

WOMAN. I was knocking.

STEVE. I see that.

WOMAN. Steven, right?

STEVE. Right.

WOMAN. Uh huh. Steven, that's right. I remember. Do you remember me? I'm the manager, I live ...

STEVE. Yeah, you're the ... you live ...

WOMAN. Yeah, I live over there.

STEVE. Look, what can I do for you?

WOMAN. I took this down from up there, under the—the, uh—whatta ya call it—the overthing there.

STEVE. What?

WOMAN. I don't remember what it's called, the thing that hangs over—ya know, the ...

STEVE. I know. What is that?

WOMAN. What?

STEVE. In your hand.

WOMAN. Birdfeeder.

STEVE. A birdfeeder?

WOMAN. Yes. What does it look like?

STEVE. Well I guess it looks like a birdfeeder actually.

WOMAN. It is a birdfeeder.

STEVE. I can tell.

WOMAN. Then why did you ask me what it was?

STEVE. Well, I couldn't see what it was.

WOMAN. It's a birdfeeder. (*Pause.*) Overhang!

STEVE. Excuse me?

WOMAN. It's an overhang.

STEVE. Huh!

WOMAN. I mean it's an overhang, where I got this down from. That's what I was trying to think of ... it's ... I couldn't remember what it was called. An overhang! Overthing. Psssss stupid.

STEVE. So can I help you with something?

WOMAN. Oh yeah. I took this down and I was trying to unscrew it but I can't get it unscrewed so I thought maybe you could help me cuz I saw your light on.

STEVE. Sure thing. Let me see it.

WOMAN. Thanks. No problem. Watch out, don't spill any of that juice on your hands.

STEVE. Right.

WOMAN. I hope I didn't get you up. Did I?

STEVE. I was up.

WOMAN. I thought so, I heard music.

STEVE. It's not too loud is it?

WOMAN. Doesn't bother me. (*SHE dances.*)

STEVE. If it's too loud I can turn it down.

WOMAN. It's fine. I'm just glad I didn't get you up. (*SHE continues to dance.*)

STEVE. Not at all. (*HE watches her dance a moment.*) I think I better just turn it off.

WOMAN. Oh no, it's ...

STEVE. I didn't realize what time it is. Here you go, how's that?

WOMAN. Did you get it?

STEVE. Uh huh ...

WOMAN. Oh yeah! That's great. Thanks a lot. It's perfect. (*Goes to sink, looks out of the window , then pours the juice out of the feeder.*)

STEVE. Don't mention it.

WOMAN. I didn't think I'd get it unscrewed.

STEVE. Well there it is.

WOMAN. I know.

STEVE. Alright then.

WOMAN. You're sure I didn't get you up?

STEVE. Like I said ...

WOMAN. What are you, partying?

STEVE. No, not tonight.

WOMAN. I heard the music I thought maybe you were partying.

STEVE. Actually I was trying to study.

WOMAN. You're studying?

STEVE. I'm trying to.

WOMAN. You're studying on a Saturday night?

STEVE. 'Fraid so.

WOMAN. No you're not ... are you really?

STEVE. I'm trying to.

WOMAN. Why are you studying on a Saturday night?

STEVE. Because I've got a paper due on Monday morning.

WOMAN. Oh, what a drag.

STEVE. Yeah well ... that's—

WOMAN. I've been partying.

STEVE. I can tell.

WOMAN. What's that supposed to mean?

STEVE. You look like you've been partying.

WOMAN. You mean I look like a drunk pig?

STEVE. No, I didn't mean that at all.

WOMAN. Well, what!

STEVE. Well, you look ...

WOMAN. What! I look what?

STEVE. Well, you look ... happy.

WOMAN. Happy?

STEVE. Yeah. Like you've been having a good time.

WOMAN. I've been having a good time alright.

STEVE. It shows.

WOMAN. Yes, I've been having a real good time. I've been drinking.

STEVE. Is that right?

WOMAN. Sure, why not, it's Saturday night isn't it?

STEVE. It sure is.

WOMAN. Damn! It's cold in here!

STEVE. I know. Look I gotta get back to my writing.

WOMAN. You're a writer?

STEVE. I'm trying to be.

WOMAN. But you write, right?

STEVE. I try.

WOMAN. Can I read it?

STEVE. No. It's not finished.

WOMAN. I'm not a critic or anything. I just want to read it. I'd really like to read it if you'd let me.

STEVE. I don't let anybody read my writing until it's finished, okay?

STEVE. Maybe later.

WOMAN. Sure. I'm cold. Aren't you cold, me too ... I'm cold.

STEVE. Yeah, the heat's not on.

WOMAN. Well, why don't you turn it on?

STEVE. I tried, but the gas doesn't seem to be coming out.

WOMAN. Well, why didn't you tell my husband, he's the manager, ya know?

STEVE. I did, he was supposed to come by this morning.

WOMAN. And he didn't?

STEVE. Apparently not.

WOMAN. Are you sure you told him?

STEVE. He probably just forgot.

WOMAN. Isn't that just like Manny? (*Crosses to window and looks out.*)

STEVE. Maybe he was too busy or something, I don't know.

WOMAN. Oh, he tells good stories, makes great promises, but does he deliver?

STEVE. It's no big deal.

WOMAN. But aren't you cold?

STEVE. I'm okay. I got some sweaters and stuff.

WOMAN. You ... you ... want me to look at it for you?

STEVE. That's okay, thanks!

WOMAN. I'd really like to look at it if you'll let me.

STEVE. I've really got to get back to work here.

WOMAN. I'm just trying to help.

STEVE. I know, but this is important.

WOMAN. So's heat.

STEVE. Maybe you could just talk me through it so I know how.

WOMAN. Here hold this will ya? No wait, no, I'll just set it down right here. (*Sets feeder down on floor. Goes over, bends over and looks at the heater.*)

STEVE. See, I couldn't get the pilot to light. (*Follows her to the heater.*)

WOMAN. Nope it's not lit.

STEVE. Do you know how to get the gas going? I pressed the knob down and turned it but it didn't seem to come out.

WOMAN. I'm the manager. I've done this before. Can I wash my hands? I got that birdfeeder juice all over my hands.

STEVE. You bet, that bathroom's right there.

WOMAN. I know, I've been in here before. Don't you remember I showed you this place. (*Goes in the bathroom, leaving the bathroom door open, and starts to wash her hands.*)

STEVE. I remember.

WOMAN. You remember? Do you like it?

STEVE. Yeah, I like it.

WOMAN. So you think it's small?

STEVE. It's not bad. I don't have a lot of stuff.

WOMAN. Do you think it's cheap?

STEVE. It's pretty reasonable actually.

WOMAN. Do you think I'm fat?

STEVE. What?

WOMAN. You didn't hear me?

STEVE. I'm not sure.

WOMAN. Never mind. Do you like the toilet seat?

STEVE. The toilet seat?

WOMAN. Yeah, this contour padded one.

STEVE. It's alright I guess, ya know, as far as toilet seats go.

WOMAN. Manny gave me one for my birthday.

STEVE. That's sweet ...

WOMAN. But do you think he installed it? No. My birthday is in July, you hear that? JULY! This is November already. It's nice too, turquoise blue with silver trim around the edge right here. Oops! I dropped the towel. I got it. (*SHE comes out of the bathroom.*) I like this stuff in here. (*Looking at tapestry.*) This is nice. Do you decorate?

STEVE. No, I just kinda put it up, ya know, make it comfortable.

WOMAN. The guy next door "decorates." You ever been over there?

STEVE. No.

WOMAN. Oh. My friend used to live here but it didn't look this nice. It's never looked this nice—and believe me, I've seen it a lot of times. I'm the manager.

STEVE. I thought your husband was the manager.

WOMAN. Well, yeah, but I'm the manager too cuz he's my husband and we're both the manager, so I have all the keys.

STEVE. Well that makes sense.

WOMAN. I can come into these apartments anytime I want.

STEVE. I know.

WOMAN. You know it?

STEVE. Uh huh.

WOMAN. Good. My friend used to live here in this apartment. She moved.

STEVE. Yeah. I haven't seen her in here.

WOMAN. No, she moved. Albuquerque ... some guy. So you wouldn't, ya know, see her in here.

STEVE. I know.

WOMAN. And why would she be in here if you were in here?

STEVE. I was joking.

WOMAN. Oh.

(Pause.)

STEVE. So do you think you can get the heater going?

WOMAN. I don't know. I guess I could try ... Do you want me to look at it?

STEVE. You don't have to.

WOMAN. No, no, I'll do it. Oh yeah! OK. (*SHE bends over at the waist to look at the heater. SHE stays in this position for some time until SHE begins laughing hysterically.*) Ohhh ho ho ho. I get it!

STEVE. What?

WOMAN. That's funny ... you haven't seen her in here. Ha, ha, you're funny! You know that?

STEVE. Yeah, thanks.

WOMAN. Is your story funny?—I'll bet it is.

STEVE. I hope not.

WOMAN. Ha, ha! I'd really like to read it. Can I read it?

STEVE. No, like I said, I don't let any ...

WOMAN. Okay, okay, will you just tell me what it's about?

STEVE. It's hard to say.

WOMAN. Well, come on, does it have people in it? Or animals? Or what?

STEVE. People and animals, actually.

WOMAN. Is it a true story?

STEVE. No, it's fictitious.

WOMAN. Fictitious? Like Scooby-Doo or something?

STEVE. A little closer to Gentle Ben, I'm afraid.

WOMAN. Oh, I hate that show. Manny watches it all the time. Why do you want to write about Gentle Ben?

STEVE. I don't want to write about Gentle Ben, believe me.

WOMAN. Then why are ya?

STEVE. Look, it's not about Gentle Ben. (*Quickly.*) It's about a philosophy professor at a university, who gets fed up with the rat race of the modern world and goes to live in the woods where he finds this bear that has his foot caught in a trap, and so he helps the bear get out of the trap and they begin to communicate with each other, and the man reaches a balance between nature and social code.

(*Pause.*)

WOMAN. You ever notice how Gentle Ben never takes a dump? (*Pause.*) Huh?

STEVE. I've never really thought about it to tell you the truth.

WOMAN. Heck, he eats a lot of food and they let him in the house a lot; and he's never once taken a dump on the floor?

STEVE. Good point. Now look, about the heater, you want to just forget about it. We can do ...

WOMAN. No, I'll do it! I said I'd do it, I'll do it. I ain't like Manny!—if I say ...

STEVE. It's not really necessary, I can ...

WOMAN. Do you have some matches?

STEVE. Right next to the heater on the floor.

WOMAN. Oh, yeah. Okay. (*Picks up the matches.*) If you wait for Manny you'll wait till August. (*Bends over.*) OK. (*Pause.*) Man runs

from responsibility like a ... Okay. Okay.   ...
he's never here ... Can I ask you a question,
Steve?

STEVE. Shoot.

WOMAN. Why does your professor guy leave?

STEVE. So he can figure out his life.

WOMAN. He lives in the city?

STEVE. Yes.

WOMAN. So why does he leave?

STEVE. To get away from the distractions of
his daily life.

WOMAN. But that is his life.

STEVE. Presently, yes.

WOMAN. Well if he wants to figure it out, why
doesn't he stay?

STEVE. He wants to put some distance on it.

WOMAN. Huh. What about his wife? What's
she supposed to do while he's fuckin' around in the
woods?

STEVE. The guy's not married.

WOMAN. Then what's he running away
from?

STEVE. Look, the guy is not running away,
okay? And he's got like a girlfriend or ...
something.

WOMAN. What did she do?

STEVE. She doesn't really enter into the story.

WOMAN. That figures. So what happens?

STEVE. Like I said, he meets this bear.

WOMAN. I mean when he comes back.

STEVE. I'm not sure if he does come back.

WOMAN. He's gotta come back.

STEVE. Why?

WOMAN. 'Cause that's why he left. You said he wanted to figure out his life.

STEVE. Yeah, so he can decide if he wants to live there.

WOMAN. Then he shouldn't leave. How the hell's he gonna know if he wants to live there unless he lives there?

(Pause. STEVE glances at his notes.)

STEVE. It's very complicated.

WOMAN. It seems simple to me. The guy's not too bright, huh?

STEVE. That could very well be it.

WOMAN. Hey, you want to write a real good story?

STEVE. I'm trying.

WOMAN. You should write one about me.

STEVE. I've got enough troubles with this one right now.

WOMAN. It'd be easy. See, I moved to Colorado a while ago, and when I came back everything was the same. Exactly the same, ya know?

STEVE. The people or the place or what?

WOMAN. The people, the place, everything. I mean, sure, you can go away and leave, but when you come back everything is the same. It's not like it used to be. It's boring.

STEVE. You just said it was the same.

WOMAN. Yeah, it is, except it's different, cuz before it was all new, but now it's ... What?

STEVE. The same?

WOMAN. Yeah, at first we were moving towards something in a way, like some day I would just kinda got there and then everything would be like great, but then ya get there and it's— this is it? I mean, stuff keeps getting in the way that you have to deal with, like ... I don't know ... life I guess.

STEVE. Well, you just gotta keep on trying. You know?

WOMAN. I know, but ... I know.

STEVE. Speaking of which, what about the heater? Let's just forget it, okay?

WOMAN. I can't even see it to tell you the truth.

STEVE. Alright, that's fine.

WOMAN. Are you mad?

STEVE. No, I'm not mad; I should just get back to my work. So thanks.

WOMAN. Here, I know, here, you can start the oven. Do you have those matches? (*SHE goes into the kitchen, opens oven.*)

STEVE. I'll just wait until tomorrow.

WOMAN. Here they are.

STEVE. That's expensive.

WOMAN. Don't worry, we pay for the gas. Anyways, it's Manny's fault it isn't on.

STEVE. Well, maybe for a while to warm things up.

WOMAN. Keep it on as long as you want. (*Lights oven. Begins to waft air toward him.*) Feel that? It's warm, huh?

STEVE. Listen, I appreciate it.

WOMAN. Anytime. I like to help. But Manny doesn't let me. Says I'm too stupid. Do you think I'm stupid?

STEVE. No.

WOMAN. Really? Do you think I'm smart?

STEVE. You're very resourceful.

WOMAN. What's that mean?

STEVE. Like how you turned the oven on. That was very smart.

WOMAN. Thanks.

STEVE. You're welcome.

(Pause. SHE goes to the window and looks out.)

WOMAN. God, I can't believe I'm in here.

STEVE. Me neither.

WOMAN. I watch you sometimes. Uh huh, I do. Do you watch me?

STEVE. I've seen you around.

WOMAN. You know what I mean?

STEVE. Look, I have a lot of writing to do.

WOMAN. Do it tomorrow.

STEVE. I'll have to, but I still got more to do tonight if I want it to be any good.

WOMAN. I'm sure it's good. I can tell.

STEVE. No, actually I think it may be a piece of shit.

WOMAN. It is. I can tell, I mean, good you know, not a ... Want me to help? (*Goes to type-writer.*)

STEVE. No! Thanks though. But you've done quite enough with the heat. So I should ...

WOMAN. I'm a good speller.

STEVE. I'm sure you are.

WOMAN. Ask me to spell something.

STEVE. How about toodle loo.

WOMAN. Toodle loo. Oh, okay.

STEVE. What the hell are you doing?

WOMAN. Typing toodle loo.

STEVE. Leave it alone! I'm having enough trouble with it already, I don't need you typing on it!

WOMAN. What are you yelling for?

STEVE. You're typing on my story!

WOMAN. Then why'd you ask me to spell toodle loo?

STEVE. I didn't want you to type toodle loo, I want you to toodle loo.

WOMAN. Well, you don't have to yell. I'm just trying to help.

STEVE. I didn't mean to yell but look I gotta write this thing and ...

WOMAN. Forget it! Okay?—just forget it! (*Starts to leave.*) I don't know what you think I'm doing here, but I only wanted to talk to somebody and your lights were on. So I wanted to talk to you, except you're not talking.

STEVE. It's nothing personal, I just got my mind on my homework.

WOMAN. I don't think anybody around here parties anymore, except the guy next to you but he's a 'mo ... and this guy on the other side, he parties alright, but he's ... well, never mind what he is ... believe me he partied till he broke his arm. This was before you lived here. He broke his arm right in two.

STEVE. Well I guess that will happen when you're partying.

WOMAN. No! Don't you party?—It was an accident. Manny did it because he said I got a nice ass and Manny heard him and was drunk and so he pushed him into the wall and his arm went crack.

STEVE. That's a little severe don't you think?

WOMAN. You think so?

STEVE. Well the guy was probably drunk himself.

WOMAN. You mean he'd have to be drunk to say I have a nice ass?

STEVE. I didn't mean that at all.

WOMAN. Do you?

STEVE. Do I?

WOMAN. Think it's nice.

STEVE. Your ass?

WOMAN. Do you think I have a nice ass?

STEVE. Well I've never really looked at it to tell you the truth.

WOMAN. Well look at it.

STEVE. I should get back to my writing here.

WOMAN. What's the matter? Too fat for you or something?

STEVE. Who says it's fat?

WOMAN. Manny says it's fat. He calls me lard ass.

STEVE. Guys just say that stuff, they don't mean it.

WOMAN. Then you like it?

STEVE. What's like?

WOMAN. Just look! Please! I won't tell Manny.

STEVE. Promise?

WOMAN. Promise. Look.

(Long pause.)

STEVE. It's very attractive.

WOMAN. You're just saying that.

STEVE. Would I lie?

WOMAN. You really think it's nice?

STEVE. On my honor!

WOMAN. Thank you.

STEVE. You're welcome.

WOMAN. Of course I had a kid, that didn't help any.

STEVE. You can't tell.

WOMAN. I try to do my squats everyday. They help.

STEVE. I see.

WOMAN. You sure you don't want to party?

STEVE. No. I have to get back to this now, okay?

WOMAN. Okay. I'm leaving. I really like this thing above the bed. What is it?

STEVE. Tapestry.

WOMAN. Tapestry? Mind if I look at it? Just for a second? You just write. (*SHE lays in bed.*) I like the way it hangs down like that. It looks like a balloon. This bed is so soft. It makes me wanna take my clothes off and crawl under the covers.

STEVE. You don't want to do that.

WOMAN. I didn't say I was gonna. I just said it makes me want to. Jeez ... relax, you little puppy.

STEVE. Look, I got a lot to do.

(*Pause.*)

WOMAN. What would you do if I took my clothes off?

STEVE. You won't.

WOMAN. How about if I just unbuttoned my shirt a little? (*SHE starts to slowly unbutton her shirt.*)

STEVE. Please don't do that.

WOMAN. What's the matter, are you scared? Don't like breasts or something?

STEVE. I love breasts. But you're a married woman.

WOMAN. I'm married to a pig. You call that married?

STEVE. That's not the point.

WOMAN. Don't worry about Manny, he's at the bar still. He's been at the bar every night since last Saturday. He never looks at them anyway. Look here, you like 'em? I can do this.

STEVE. (*Crossing to her.*) I think it's time for you to leave.

WOMAN. (*Slaps him.*) Don't tell me when it's time for me to leave. I'm the manager.

STEVE. Will you please leave?

WOMAN. I'll leave when I'm good and ready and not a minute before, you understand?

(*Long pause.*)

STEVE. When do you think that will be?

WOMAN. Right now, Mr. Smarty Pants college boy. Don't go flattering yourself into thinking I would stay here with you. (*Pause.*) I'm sorry. I didn't mean to ruin your night.

STEVE. You didn't ruin my night. Okay?

WOMAN. Okay. Will you just hold me? No? (*Pause.*) Just for a second? (*Pause.*) I'm a cow, huh? (*WOMAN exits then quickly re-enters.*) There's a car coming into the driveway.

STEVE. So what?

WOMAN. So what if it's Manny?

STEVE. Shit! (*Looking out. Matter-of-factly.*) It's my girlfriend. Great.

WOMAN. Your girlfriend?

STEVE. Uh huh. Now will you get out of here?

WOMAN. She'll see me.

STEVE. Don't worry about it; I'll explain everything. Shit, shit, shit.

WOMAN. Won't she be mad that there's a woman in your apartment?

STEVE. You figure it out. There's this guy, right? And he's got this girlfriend who's already a little upset cuz he doesn't call and then he tells her she can't come over because he has to write and she gets there and he has a woman in his apartment.

WOMAN. I'd kill you. (*SHE runs into the bathroom.*)

STEVE. What the hell are you doing?

WOMAN. I'm gonna hide in the bathroom so she won't see me.

STEVE. Don't be ridiculous.

WOMAN. She won't know I'm here.

STEVE. Come out of there—what if she has to go to the bathroom, numb nuts?

WOMAN. I'll hide in the shower.

STEVE. (*Goes to door and tries to open it.*) This is totally unnecessary, now get out of there, will you?

WOMAN. Be quiet or she'll hear you.

(*There is a KNOCK at the door.*)

STEVE. (*Fully exasperated.*) Come on, this is stupid. People don't hide unless there's a reason. You hear me? This is *stupid*. Only a real stupid person would do this kind of thing.

SHELLY. (*Off.*) Steve.

STEVE. Coming! You're going to go through with this? Thanks a lot. Thanks a fucking lot. You're a moron, you understand? An imbecile. A pin head.

SHELLY. (*Off.*) I just gotta talk to you for a minute and then I'll leave.

STEVE. Come in. It's open.

SHELLY. No, it's locked.

(STEVE looks at the bathroom door then goes and opens the front door.)

SHELLY. Why didn't you answer the door?

STEVE. There's a woman in my bathroom.

SHELLY. And a midget and a mule, I know.

STEVE. No, just a woman. Listen Shelly, you trust me, right?

SHELLY. Of course I trust you. I just wondered why you didn't answer.

STEVE. Would you believe this?—I'm sitting here writing and this woman comes knocking at my door ...

STEVE. I didn't want you to come over.

SHELLY. Fine, I'll leave.

STEVE. No. I want you to stay. We gotta take care of this.

SHELLY. I know we do. I brought some wine, Steven.

STEVE. I see that. So this woman comes knocking at my door with some *thing* in her hand...

SHELLY. We don't have to drink it.

STEVE. Then why'd you bring it?

SHELLY. So I could tell you that I would leave you alone. *(Pause.)* I'm freezing.

STEVE. Well come in.

SHELLY. Are you sure?

STEVE. Sure. So this woman comes barging in with this birdfeeder in her hand ...

SHELLY. Birdfeeder? This is expensive wine.

STEVE. I'm not talking about the wine, Shelly, I'm talking about the woman in my apartment.

SHELLY. I know. You're trying to study.

STEVE. Well, yeah.

SHELLY. How's it coming?

STEVE. It's not coming at all right now. Leave it alone.

SHELLY. I'm not going to read it. Relax.

STEVE. It's not finished.

SHELLY. Well, what's it about?

STEVE. About eighteen, nineteen pages. Shelly, I really wish you'd listen to me.

SHELLY. I do listen!

STEVE. Well it sure doesn't seem like you've heard what I said.

SHELLY. There's a woman in your house and you want her to leave, right?

STEVE. Right. It doesn't seem to have an effect on you; don't you care? I mean, you must be mad or something. Are you mad?

SHELLY. Steven, I'm not mad. I feel pretty stupid. Okay?

STEVE. Well I don't blame you. Look, the woman's bombed.

SHELLY. I look drunk?

STEVE. Why, are you drunk?

SHELLY. Okay, so I'm a little drunk.

STEVE. Why are you drunk?

SHELLY. It's Saturday night, isn't it?

STEVE. It sure is.

SHELLY. Remember this wine, Steven?

STEVE. I sure do?

SHELLY. We don't have to drink it.

STEVE. I'd love to. But first ...

SHELLY. I'm sorry.

STEVE. Why are you sorry?

SHELLY. About the phone call, I was being a baby and it was totally uncalled for ...

STEVE. You weren't being a baby you ...

SHELLY. Yes I was, and you really didn't want me to come over ...

STEVE. I know, I know. I'm not mad.

SHELLY. Steven, you are, I can tell.

STEVE. Well, yeah!—but that's because ...

SHELLY. I know you hate it when I act like that and I try not to, but I ...

STEVE. I know, baby, I'm not mad about the phone call I'm mad about this woman in my house...

SHELLY. Steven, just let me say what I have to say and then we can get the woman out of here. Okay?

STEVE. Okay, but ... Okay.

SHELLY. You want a glass of wine? It'll just take a second.

STEVE. No, Shelly, I want to get this taken care of right now.

SHELLY. I'm talking, I'm talking. So anyway I was driving over here and I started thinking about the phone call and everything and how I wanted to come over and you not wanting me to ...

STEVE. I wanted you to, I always want to see you ...

SHELLY. I know you want to, but you were writing and I know how important this class is to you and how we talked about Thursday that you had to finish it this weekend, and I wasn't gonna bother you at all until you called but you never did call and I want you to do it, I really do cuz you're good, you really are, even though you don't think so sometimes and you get frustrated and I know I'm going to have to get used to it cuz it's what you're going to be doing, but I get frustrated too, I think that's why I picked up the bottle of wine, no, I know that's why, because I knew you'd be upset and I didn't want it to be a negative thing for us, especially you, so I thought I'd get a fancy bottle of wine, come over and give you a kiss and tell you I love you and leave, or fuck your brains out if that's what you wanted because I don't want to be doing this sort of thing every time you lock yourself up, but I get jealous, even though I know you're not with anybody else but sometimes you don't call and I get mad cuz you say you will, and I wait, and then when you do call you never talk, and I know I don't help and I'm sorry, (*SHELLY sits in Steve's lap.*) but you never talk to me about what's going on with you and I'm trying to understand and I'm sorry and I won't do it again I promise and I know I've said it before but this time I mean it.

STEVE. Are you finished?

SHELLY. Yes. I just wanted to tell you how I feel. Do you love me?

(SHE starts to get up. STEVE holds her there.)

STEVE. Baby, baby, baby come here. *(HE brings her to him.)*

SHELLY. You feel so good.

STEVE. You too.

SHELLY. I missed you.

STEVE. Me too.

SHELLY. Mmm.

STEVE. Mmm hmm.

SHELLY. Mmm. Let's do it.

STEVE. Later. We'll do it later. Leave my pants alone.

SHELLY. You never want to do it anymore.

STEVE. We do it all the time.

SHELLY. No, we used to do it all the time, now you want to *write* all the time.

STEVE. Listen—

SHELLY. I'm listening.

STEVE. You're not listening, you're undoing my pants.

SHELLY. I'll you know what. *(SHE drops to her knees.)*

STEVE. I don't want you to you know what. Cut it out, Shelly.

SHELLY. You always want me to you know what.

STEVE. I don't ALWAYS.

SHELLY. Steven!

STEVE. Well that's 'cause you never do it.

SHELLY. I do it all the time.

STEVE. Shelly!

SHELLY. Well, I do it a lot.

STEVE. I know you do ... it.

SHELLY. A lot.

STEVE. And you do it well.

SHELLY. You don't think so.

STEVE. I do too.

SHELLY. Sit down and lay back.

STEVE. (*Still standing above her.*) Shelly, stop it!

SHELLY. You don't have to do anything.

STEVE. I'm not going to do anything and neither are you, now quit it, let go of him! Listen to me.

(There is the sound of the WOMAN vomiting coming from the bathroom.)

SHELLY. What is that?

STEVE. What?

SHELLY. Sounds like somebody throwing up in your bathroom.

STEVE. It does, doesn't it?

SHELLY. Is there somebody in your bathroom?

STEVE. Bingo.

SHELLY. You got a woman in your bathroom?

STEVE. Double fucking bingo.

SHELLY. Double fucking bingo? What the hell does that mean?

STEVE. It means there's a woman in my bathroom.

SHELLY. And all you got to say is double bingo? I feel like a pig. Why didn't you tell me?

STEVE. What are you talking about?—I did tell you. Shelly, how drunk are ...

SHELLY. You son of a bitch! What the hell is she doing in there?

STEVE. She's hiding.

SHELLY. May I ask why she's hiding?

STEVE. She saw your car pull up and she thought you'd kill me.

SHELLY. Why would she think that?

STEVE. She's an idiot.

SHELLY. That doesn't satisfy my curiosity, Steven. What were you doing?

STEVE. Look, the lady's bombed.

SHELLY. *She's* bombed?

STEVE. She forced her way in here and then wouldn't leave. Just ask the woman, she'll tell you.

SHELLY. (*Goes to the door and tries to open it.*) Would you ask her to come out?

STEVE. You're standing there ask her yourself.

SHELLY. (*Knocks.*) Will you open this door?

(*There is no response.*)

STEVE. Come on, she knows you're in there.

SHELLY. What are you doing in there?

WOMAN. I'm getting sick.

SHELLY. Beside the obvious. What are you doing in his apartment?

WOMAN. I just wanted someone to talk to.

STEVE. She wanted me to unscrew her birdfeeder.
SHELLY. Her *birdfeeder*?

(Pause HE gets feeder.)

STEVE. You wanna tell her about the birdfeeder?
WOMAN. Oh yeah. The feeder.
SHELLY. Is this your birdfeeder?
WOMAN. He just wanted it for himself.
STEVE. What!
SHELLY. What does she mean by that?
STEVE. I haven't got a clue.
SHELLY. What do you mean by that?
WOMAN. Forget it.
STEVE. What did I ever do to you, woman, you wanna tell me that?

(WOMAN vomits.)

SHELLY. So this is what you do when you tell me you're writing?
STEVE. I was writing. Look. (*Goes to the kitchen table and picks up pages and shows them to her.*)
SHELLY. Eighteen, nineteen pages. I left you alone for two days and that's it?
STEVE. This is good stuff. It's quality, not quantity.
SHELLY. I don't call this writing, do you?
STEVE. No, I call this sitting around bitching.

SHELLY. I think I have a right to bitch a little, Steven. I felt stupid about being jealous and I get here and you have some drunk pig in your bathroom.

STEVE. Don't call her a pig.

SHELLY. Don't call her a pig? You're worried I'm gonna hurt her feelings? What about mine?

WOMAN. Who you calling a pig?

SHELLY. You got someone in there with you? (To Steve.) I feel like I've had my guts kicked out.

STEVE. Look, you trust me, don't you?

SHELLY. What am I supposed to think?

STEVE. You know I'm not interested in anybody but you.

SHELLY. How would I know that? I never see you.

STEVE. When you do see me, Shelly.

SHELLY. I don't know anymore, Steven. What about the redhead that's always hanging on you?

STEVE. She doesn't hang on me. I'm her tutor.

SHELLY. I've seen the way she looks at you.

STEVE. She knows I'm going out with you.

SHELLY. You better believe she knows. I'd like to poke her eyes out.

STEVE. So she looks at me. You don't see me looking at anybody do you?

SHELLY. Yes I do.

STEVE. Come on, Shelly.

SHELLY. No, you come on, Steven. What about the blonde?

STEVE. What blonde?

SHELLY. You know what blonde I'm talking about. The one with the gopher patch sewed on the ass of her pants.

STEVE. Joan?

SHELLY. Joan, Jezebel. I don't know, the one in our biology class.

STEVE. It's a ground hog.

SHELLY. I don't care if it's a laboratory rat, and how do you know it's a ground hog anyway?

STEVE. *I don't* know—somebody told me.

SHELLY. I've seen you looking at it.

STEVE. No you haven't.

SHELLY. Yes I have. When you don't think I'm looking at you, you look at her ass. I've seen.

STEVE. Then why didn't you say anything?

SHELLY. Because you're trying so hard to be sly about it.

STEVE. Look, can we get this woman out of the bathroom.

SHELLY. Don't change the subject.

STEVE. Okay, so I look at Joan's ass once in a while. So what?

SHELLY. So you said you didn't.

STEVE. So I lied.

SHELLY. So you lied—and you want me to trust you?

STEVE. Just because I look at her ass doesn't mean I want to do anything.

SHELLY. Then why look?

STEVE. I can't help it. You see an ass go by, you look at it.

SHELLY. I don't.

STEVE. You're not a man.

SHELLY. What does that have to do with anything?

STEVE. It's instinctual. It's directly linked to the human natural attraction to beauty. And some men are ass men, and some men are ... tit men. I can't believe I just said ...

SHELLY. I guess that makes you an ass man?

STEVE. I have an appreciation for the female bottom, yes. That doesn't mean I ...

SHELLY. Is it nice?

STEVE. Is what nice?

SHELLY. Her ass. Is it nice?

STEVE. What am I an expert all of a sudden?

SHELLY. You're an ass man, you must have some opinion.

STEVE. What difference does it make?

SHELLY. It's nice, isn't it?

STEVE. This is ridiculous. Why are you drunk?

SHELLY. My being drunk has nothing to with this.

STEVE. I just wish you weren't drunk. I have a feeling we wouldn't be having this conversation ...

SHELLY. He kept buying me drinks.

STEVE. Who was buying you drinks?

SHELLY. Robert.

STEVE. Why was Robert buying you drinks?

SHELLY. If I thought it would make you jealous I wouldn't have gone.

STEVE. You know he just wants to get in your pants.

SHELLY. That's not true.

STEVE. Now who's lying?

SHELLY. Well that's not what I want. I just wanted to talk to someone.

STEVE. You're talking to Robert about me?

SHELLY. No.

STEVE. Oh.

SHELLY. Are you jealous?

STEVE. Should I be?

SHELLY. No.

STEVE. Then I'm not.

SHELLY. Why not?

STEVE. Do you want me to be?

SHELLY. No, I just want to know why you're not.

STEVE. Because I trust you, Shelly.

SHELLY. I think some drunk pig hiding in the bathroom is worse than some guy buying me drinks.

STEVE. Stop calling her a pig, would you?

WOMAN. You can't talk to me that way.

STEVE. Shelly, do you trust me?

SHELLY. Do you think I have a nice ass?

WOMAN. I'm the manager.

SHELLY. Congratulations, you oinker.

STEVE. You're being stupid, Shelly.

SHELLY. I don't think it's stupid, I just want to know how I compare with other women.

STEVE. Shelly, this isn't really about your ass, is it?

SHELLY. No. Answer the question.

STEVE. You have the nicest ass I've ever laid hands on.

SHELLY. What about your eyes?

STEVE. Eyes, ears, nose and throat. I worship it, I adore it, I want to marry it, okay?

SHELLY. You don't have to say that.

STEVE. Okay, it's huge, it's massive, I've seen whales with smaller butts.

SHELLY. You don't have to be a dick about it.

WOMAN. You cow.

STEVE. What do I have to do, build a shrine to it before you trust me?

SHELLY. Steven, she just called me a cow.

STEVE. Well, you called her an oinker, Shelly. Now listen, I've been writing, okay ...

WOMAN. Mooo ...

STEVE. ... this woman comes over bombed ...

SHELLY. Don't you moo at me, you sow.

STEVE. ... and wants me to unscrew her birdfeeder ...

WOMAN. moo ...

STEVE. ... fix my heater ...

SHELLY. oink ...

STEVE. ... tell me her life story ...

WOMAN. moo ...

STEVE. ... she saw your lights and ...

SHELLY. oink ...

STEVE. ... thought you were her husband ...

(SHELLY and WOMAN continue to moo and oink throughout the following.)

STEVE. ... thought you were her husband ... flipped her fuckin' wig ... and ran into the damn bathroom. Now that's what happened. You can believe it or not. I just want to get back to my writing! Hey! Can we knock off Old MacDonald here?!?!

(Pause. THEY quiet down.)

STEVE. Shelly, you're being ridiculous.
SHELLY. You got a woman hiding in your bathroom and I'm being ridiculous?
STEVE. You're oinking at her, Shelly. You're oinking.
SHELLY. Yeah, and she's mooing back.
STEVE. That's not the point.
SHELLY. Get her out of there, Steven.
WOMAN. He said I have a very attractive ass.
SHELLY. Is that true?
STEVE. She put it right in my face, what was I supposed to do?
SHELLY. I'm leaving. (*Goes to the front door.*) Don't worry I won't bother you anymore.
STEVE. Don't go. Please. I was writing.
SHELLY. (*Stops in doorway.*) You wanna write a real good story? You should write one about me, all about a girl who goes out with this guy who says he has to write and all the time he's got a woman in his house.
STEVE. Shelly, what do you want from me?
SHELLY. I want a relationship with stability.

STEVE. Jesus, don't start this.

SHELLY. I want to be able to depend on you.

STEVE. I can't handle this right now.

SHELLY. When are you going to be able to handle it, huh?

STEVE. Can we get the woman out of the bathroom?

SHELLY. No. I want an answer. (*Slams door.*) I've bent over backwards for this relationship.

STEVE. I know you have.

SHELLY. And you give me nothing in return.

STEVE. (*Stunned.*) What do you want me to say?

SHELLY. I shouldn't have to tell you.

STEVE. What, I'm supposed to guess?

SHELLY. No, you're supposed to know. Nothing to say, Steven? (*Pause.*) Fine. (*SHE starts to leave.*)

STEVE. Shelly, I told you I need to spend some time with this writing.

SHELLY. I know, but what am I supposed to do while you're fucking around with these stupid stories?

STEVE. They're not stupid.

SHELLY. No, they're Pulitzer Prize winners.

STEVE. I didn't say that.

SHELLY. No, you never say anything. One teacher tells you you might have some talent and you give up everything else in your life.

STEVE. I'm not doing this for him. I'm doing it for me.

SHELLY. What about me?

STEVE. What about you?

SHELLY. (*Hurt.*) What if you don't make it, Steven?

STEVE. I don't want to think about that right now.

SHELLY. When are you going to think about it, huh? Do you know how many people actually make it? Do you have any idea?

STEVE. Yes, I know. Believe me.

SHELLY. (*Hurtful.*) Very few, Steven.

(*Beat.*)

STEVE. So now you know why I'm sitting here writing on a Saturday night.

SHELLY. I didn't mean it that way ...

STEVE. That's okay, just go ahead and go.

SHELLY. You didn't want me to come over here, you never want to see me, I get here and you got a woman with an attractive ass hiding in your bathroom ...

STEVE. Alright, alright, just get the hell out.

SHELLY. I'll leave when I'm good and ready.

STEVE. Get out you cow.

SHELLY. Don't you ever call me a cow. Ever.

STEVE. Moo. Moo.

SHELLY. Jesus, Steven, what's happening to you? (*HE continues mooing.*) You're mooing at me, Steven! You're mooing.

(SHE starts to cry. After a moment, STEVEN goes over and attempts to comfort her by putting his arms around her.)

STEVE. I'm sorry, baby, I didn't mean ...
SHELLY. Don't touch me!

(SHE slaps him in the face and leaves, slamming door. After a moment HE looks at the bathroom door.)

STEVE. You wanna tell me what I did to you, woman? This is the thanks I get for doing you a favor?
WOMAN. Nobody calls me a pig except me. *(Flushes TOILET.)*
STEVE. Fine. That's ah ... that's fine. Um, do you think you could leave now? Huh? I mean, you've ruined my relationship, isn't that enough for one night? Are you listening to me in there?
WOMAN. Yeah, I hear you. You're just like Manny! I didn't ruin your relationship, you did. You never should have called her a cow.
STEVE. Ha, ha, ha. *(Screaming.)* I hope you choke on your own vomit! You hear me? Now get out! Hey ... *(There is a KNOCK on the door.)* ... I'm talking to you. What do I owe you, back fuckin' rent or something ... *(Heading toward front door.)* ... something I don't know about *(Opening door.)* ... Just get the hell out of here, will ya?
MANNY. *(Standing in the doorway.)* You want your faced punched in?

STEVE. No.

MANNY. Then you watch your mouth, little buddy.

STEVE. I'm sorry. I didn't know it was you ...

MANNY. What's all the ruckus? You're going to wake the whole goddamn complex with all this noise.

STEVE. I'm having some serious problems here, Manny.

MANNY. I'll say. I saw your woman peeling out of here like hell on wheels. What's she think she is, king of the road?

STEVE. She's just upset, it won't happen again.

MANNY. It better not. She's liable to run someone down. We got kids around here, you know? How do you think she'd feel if she flattened a child, huh? Not that I'd mind, mind you, I'd kinda like to see that myself. Little shits! But it wouldn't look good, if you get my drift.

STEVE. I'm right with you, pal. Listen, I'm glad you're here, I need your help. Come in.

MANNY. Sure, hell why not, it ain't like I'm in any hurry to get home and fight with my little woman. Brewski? (*MANNY enters and looks around, goes to the window, looks out, then notices the tapestry.*) Hey! Fancy schmancy! Looks like a love palace in here, whatta ya call that thing above the bed there?

STEVE. It's just a tapestry.

MANNY. Looks like one of those Arabian whatchamajigs. (*HE goes over and feels the bed.*) Soft! (*HE sits on the bed.*) Mind?

STEVE. Go right ahead, make yourself comfortable. I need to talk to you about something, Manny.

MANNY. Girl problems?

STEVE. In a way.

MANNY. Well, I don't know how much help I can be. I'm married you know. But I'll give a listen. Hey, wine too. Fancy schmancy. Even a cork! What are ya, a Casanova? A jigaboo? You're not a homosexual are you?

STEVE. I'm thinking about it.

MANNY. Straight shit, no bull?

STEVE. No, I was joking. I just have a tapestry above my bed.

MANNY. I was gonna say, damn, anybody who's got a girl like yours who's a 'mo deserves to have sex with a man. Am I right? Tapestry, huh? Boy, I'd bet the wife'd get a kick outta this. But, me, well ... I don't know. Tell me, this kind a thing work? All this rigamaroo? So, the girls really go for this, you get lotsa chicks?

STEVE. Look, I have a girlfriend.

MANNY. Say no more, say no more, little buddy. We're both men, right? Hey, look! Mind if I use your fingernail clippers here? I ain't seen mine in months. *Little shit.* I'll clip 'em into the ashtray, if that's alright with you.

STEVE. Oh, by all means, be my guest, clip away pal, I wouldn't have it any—Watch out for the ...

(MANNY steps on the birdfeeder.)

STEVE. ... birdfeeder.

MANNY. Aw, shit! I broke it didn't I? I'm sorry, little buddy. You let me in your house and I break your gear. Tell ya the truth I'm a little drunk.

STEVE. Why not, it's Saturday night isn't it?

MANNY. It sure is! (*Referring to the feeder.*) This is a nice one too. You a birdwatcher?

STEVE. No, it isn't actually mine.

MANNY. Damn, somebody is gonna be pretty pissed at you. I tell you what, let me pay you for it, eh?

STEVE. That won't be necessary.

MANNY. The hell it ain't. Now I insist. (*Goes for his wallet.*) I got one of these myself, you know. I think mine's a little nicer though. Well hell, 'course it is, it ain't broken. It ain't mine either, technically. It's the little woman's. I picked it up for her birthday back ... oh ... oh back ... oh hell, I don't know, back whenever her birthday was a couple years back there. (*Slaps money on table.*)

STEVE. July.

MANNY. Exactly my point. July, January, what's the big dif, huh, like the date's etched into my skull or something? It's called I remembered you were born, okay?—here's your damn gift now get off my back already. And she don't even like the thing! Says I only bought it cuz I wanted it for myself.

STEVE. She said what?

MANNY. I know, can you imagine? Well, okay sure, I like the thing, birds flying up and feeding right in front of your eyes, but I thought she'd like it too, ya know. I kinda thought it would be something we could do together, but no. Every time she gets mad at me she gets drunk and goes and dumps the feeder juice out of it.

STEVE. So you've never actually used it together? (*Picks up wine.*)

MANNY. Well it's a little hard to do without any feeder juice in it, ain't it? You wanna know what she got me for my last birthday? This'll tip your top. What do you think it was?

STEVE. I'm sure I don't know.

MANNY. Go ahead, guess.

STEVE. I haven't the foggiest, really.

MANNY. Come on, don't be a girl. Guess.

STEVE. A tie?

MANNY. Wrong. One down.

STEVE. Cologne?

MANNY. Not even.

STEVE. A toolbox?

MANNY. Close. One of those adult fantasy fun kits, if you know what I mean and I think you do.

STEVE. That's sweet!

MANNY. Sweet, hell. For who? What do I want with something like that? It's made up for girls.

STEVE. Maybe she wanted to get you something you could share.

MANNY. What am I gonna do with a pulsating pal?

STEVE. Pulsating pal?

MANNY. Sure. You got your pulsating pal, your veritable speed vibrator, your cuffs, belts, oils, jellies, plugs, all that stuff. It's kinky. She spends a fortune on batteries too. Says the kid gets at them toys to play space voyager, but I know that's a crock of shit. Although that kid does get into everything, no good son of a bitch. (*Goes to window. Looks out.*) Tell me, what's a woman with a kid want with that kinda stuff, huh?

STEVE. I don't know, variety maybe?

MANNY. Ah hell, would you look at me. You got your own problems right now, don't ya, little buddy? And here I am blabbering away. Go ahead. Pop! What's she want, another man?

STEVE. Who?

MANNY. Your girl.

STEVE. Shelly? No, that's not the problem at all.

MANNY. Sure? That's maybe it and she's not saying anything?

STEVE. No, Manny, that's the least of my worries right now, we're fine as far ...

MANNY. Fine shmine, I saw her leave this dump, little buddy, that ain't what I call ...

STEVE. Yeah, yeah but that was something else entirely, this has got ...

MANNY. What else is there?

STEVE. I don't want to get into that right now, okay?

MANNY. You sure she hasn't been spending time with some other feller as of lately?

STEVE. Yes, I'm sure!—well ... I mean she was at the bar with Robert tonight, but ... that's ... look I don't really want to talk about this right now, okay?

MANNY. Hey, okay! Sure! Whatever you say, pal!

STEVE. No, I'm serious. We are totally committed to each other and I ...

MANNY. I got you. That's your own personal space there.

STEVE. Listen, Manny ...

MANNY. Say no more, say no more. I mean we're both men, right?

STEVE. What exactly does that mean?

MANNY. Come on, little buddy. I've seen your woman.

STEVE. And?

MANNY. Well I hope you don't take this the wrong way, but she's a hot little number, if you know what I'm talking about and I think you do cuz she's your girl. I mean, I wouldn't mind taking a poke at her myself, if you don't mind me saying so; and I mean it as a compliment so don't go getting huffy on me. I think it's great, a guy gets a girl like that. But you gotta keep 'em happy, you hear what I'm saying? Yeah, you hear me. It's like my little woman, oh hell, we fight sometimes, sure, but she knows I ... ya know ... her in my way. Ya know, that sorta deal. I'd do damn near anything for her. (*STEVE is staring at the wine in his hand.*) 'Course it may take me a month or two to get to it sometimes. Ha ha. But I bust my ass around this dump. All these units, got ya running in five different directions! DAY AND NIGHT!! Ya always got some whiner whining about the water dripping, the bozo wants his heater lit—a fella can't light his own heater, he's got more troubles than heat, you know the type! Air conditioners, shower stalls, some ole gal wants her toilet seat changed. But I get to it eventually 'cause I know if I don't, I just might lose her. I know that!

STEVE. Yeah, but you trust her, right?

MANNY. Hell, yes. I trust her, why wouldn't I? Hey, you gonna drink this stuff, or what?

STEVE. No, I gotta study.

MANNY. You're studying on a Saturday night? No wonder you got problems with your woman. You got to take her out, show her a good time. You a pull fan?

STEVE. A what fan?

MANNY. Pull. Tractor pull.

STEVE. I've never seen one.

MANNY. You don't know what you're missing. I was at the one at the center up there last week and this engine blew, piston come flying out of there, missed this fella's head by a quarter of an inch. No bull.

STEVE. That's good, huh?

MANNY. Are you shittin' me? Can you imagine what that woulda done if it woulda hit the poor bastard? Really gets the blood flowing. You oughtta take her out to a pull, she'll love it. So will you, you don't want to be a bookworm, do ya?

STEVE. I'm not a bookworm. I just got this assignment due on Monday morning.

MANNY. What kind of assignment?

STEVE. It's a short story.

MANNY. A writer, eh?

STEVE. Student.

MANNY. Student Schmudent. You write, right?

STEVE. Right.

MANNY. Writin' down the words to be read by the people. I'm impressed. I didn't mean to call ya a bookworm. I think it's great a fella busts his butt to do what he wants to do; cuz it ain't easy either, is it?

STEVE. Sometimes it's harder than others.

MANNY. Damn straight! People always wanna get in your shit. Well, you just keep at it, you're gonna be great.

STEVE. I don't know about that.

MANNY. Sure ya are. I can tell. Prolly get yourself one a them Putzer prizes. Wouldn't that be a kick in the pants; standing up in front of all those pukes waving your surprise. And when you do I want you to remember this night here in Las Cruces, New Mexico and you remember Manny.

STEVE. I will.

MANNY. I doubt it. Oh well, no great loss there, right? MR. WRITER. Say can I take a look?

STEVE. It's not finished.

MANNY. That's all right, little buddy, I don't mind.

STEVE. It wouldn't make any sense right now.

MANNY. What do you think, I'm too stupid?

STEVE. It's not that at all, it's just ... well, it's hard to explain.

MANNY. Sure. Sure. I can take a hint. I'm not smart enough for you, huh?

STEVE. I didn't mean that at all.

MANNY. Let me tell you something, Mr. Fancy Schmancy college boy. I'm not as dumb as people seem to think I am.

STEVE. Who thinks you're dumb? Nobody thinks you're dumb.

MANNY. Oh yeah? Then how come people laugh behind my back all the time?

STEVE. Who's laughing? Nobody's laughing at you.

MANNY. You don't wanna be me do ya?

STEVE. What does that have to do with anything?

MANNY. Just answer the question.

STEVE. Well, I'd have to get all new clothes.

MANNY. Don't be stupid, you could wear mine.

STEVE. I know, Manny, I was joking.

MANNY. Well this ain't no joke, bud. I may be playing the fool but I know what I'm doing.

STEVE. I'm sure you do pal, just settle down, I didn't mean ...

MANNY. Don't tell me to settle down, BOOKWORM. I'm the Manager! Just answer the question. Do you wanna be me?

STEVE. I guess I'd have to say I'm happy being me.

MANNY. So the answer is no.

STEVE. Yes, the answer is no.

MANNY. I know. Go ahead. Laugh.

STEVE. Who's laughing at you?

MANNY. What, I ain't got eyes? People act like I can't understand them, cuz I ain't them. I got a life. I know what it's like. "Hey there's Manny, the big, dumb apartment manager. Hey come fix my toilet. Ha ha ha." Wife trampin' around. People laughin' at her. Guy next door, not the 'mo, the other guy, laughin' at her ass saying, "she's got a nice ass ... for a cow." I shoulda broke his head.

STEVE. He called her a cow?

MANNY. Aw shit man, let me tell you a story. (*Sits at table.*) You can write this down if you want to write a real good story. I was up on the roof the other day, coupla days back, last Saturday, fixing an air-conditioner, and what do you think I heard?

STEVE. I don't know. What?

MANNY. The little kids were down there teasing each other and you wanna know what they were saying? They were saying, "You're Manny, na, na, na, na, na, na." and, "No I'm not, you are. You're Manny. Ha ha." How do you think that makes a guy feel? 'Specially when his own kid's down there laughing and pointing right along with 'em.

STEVE. I'm sorry.

MANNY. No you're not.

STEVE. All right, I'm not.

MANNY. Then why say it?

STEVE. I don't know what to say.

MANNY. Then don't say nothin'.

STEVE. What do you want me to do?

MANNY. Nothing. Did I ask you to do something?

STEVE. No.

MANNY. No. (*Bangs on typewriter.*) Capital N fucking o. I don't want your pity. I may not have a college diploma, or no fancy tapestry above my bed, but I'm still a human being with the same feelings anybody else has. So you think about that next time you're trying to pass judgment on somebody. You think about that and you remember Manny.

STEVE. I will.

MANNY. I doubt it. Oh well, it's your loss. I'm going. It's plain to see I'm not good enough for the likes of you. You pussy. (*Starts out.*)

STEVE. (*Reaching out to stop him.*) Manny ...

(*MANNY grabs Steve by the shirt and raises his clenched fist as if to punch him. After a moment HE slaps Steve and exits.*)

STEVE. Jesus Christ. (*Slumps at typewriter.*)

(*After a moment, there is a loud KNOCK on the door.*)

STEVE. Come in.
SHELLY. (*Entering.*) I just came back for my wine.

(*SHE picks the wine up. STEVE doesn't answer. SHE starts to leave, but then turns back quickly into the room. MANNY enters unseen by SHELLY, grabs his beer, as SHELLY begins to speak.*)

SHELLY. Alright, let's forget about the blow job and the animal noises. I just want to try and understand this, but you gotta help me, Steven. I don't care if you look at Joan's ass. Joan's ass is not the issue. I know you're gonna look at other women. I understand that. But I don't quite understand what she is doing hiding in your bathroom. Is still in there?
STEVE. Yes.
MANNY. (*Looking at Steve and pointing to the bathroom door. HE mouths:*) You have a woman in your bathroom?
STEVE. Yes.
SHELLY. I don't suppose you want to get her out of there.

(*MANNY starts to back out door, giving Steve the "ok" sign.*)

STEVE. Manny! Come on in here, Manny.
SHELLY. What a lovely name. (*Directed to bathroom door.*) Sure, why don't you, Manny.

Maybe you can help me sort this out and tell me why my boyfriend thinks you have an attractive ass.

MANNY. Well, little buddy?

SHELLY. (*Scared, turns and sees Manny at the door.*) Ahh!! Jesus, Mary and Joseph. Who the hell are you?

MANNY. I'm Manny!—if ya don't mind.

SHELLY. Then who the hell is she?

MANNY. (*To Shelly.*) That's Joan!—as if you didn't know. (*To Steve.*) Do you?

STEVE. Do I?

MANNY. Think it's nice.

STEVE. Think what's nice?

MANNY. My ass. Do you think I have a nice ass?

STEVE. I've never looked at your ass.

MANNY. Well look at it, buddy. Nice or not?

SHELLY. Is Joan in your bathroom?

STEVE. No.

SHELLY. Are you the manager?

MANNY. Yeah, I'm the manager. You got a problem with that?

SHELLY. I thought she was the manager.

STEVE. It's his wife.

MANNY. Whose wife?

SHELLY. Is your wife the manager?

MANNY. No, I'm the manager. Who's in the bathroom, buddy?

STEVE. I'm not quite sure how to say this, Manny, buddy; but your wife. Is in the bathroom. **Manny?**

MANNY. Oh! Oh ... I gotcha, yeah! (*Thinks he gets it.*) You're in some deep shit, ain't ya?

SHELLY. Your wife's in the bathroom?

MANNY. Hold it a second, sweet cheeks. You don't think I have a nice ass, do ya, Stevo?

SHELLY. What a stupid question.

STEVE. Shelly, don't call him ...

MANNY. Stupid? You brought it up, lady.

SHELLY. I was talking about whoever's in the bathroom.

MANNY. Oh! Oh Yeah! Would you look at me? Alright then, I'm gonna turn in.

SHELLY. Wait, is your wife in the bathroom or not?

MANNY. Yeah, my wife ... Joan ... ya know, is in the bathroom. Night folks.

SHELLY. Don't you want to get your "wife" out of there?

MANNY. Oh I don't know. What do you think, Steve. You want her out of there?

STEVE. Yeah, Manny, why don't you?

MANNY. Straight shit, no bull?

STEVE. Straight shit, Manny. Get her out.

MANNY. (*Goes to the door and knocks.*) Woman, you in there?

WOMAN. (*Off.*) What do you care?

MANNY. Who's in the bathroom?

STEVE. Your wife.

MANNY. What the hell is she doing in your bathroom?

SHELLY. Hiding.

MANNY. Are you boning my wife?

STEVE. No, I'm not boning your wife!

MANNY. Woman, you better unlock this door and get your ass out here.

WOMAN. (*Off.*) Are you gonna slap me?

MANNY. No, I'm gonna kick your teeth in.

STEVE. She just wanted me to unscrew her birdfeeder.

SHELLY. At 2 o'clock in the morning.

MANNY. That's my feeder!?

STEVE. I didn't choose the time.

MANNY. Are you boning this guy?

WOMAN. (*Off.*) What if I am?

STEVE. But you're not.

MANNY. I'm gonna kill you, woman.

(During the following STEVE begins to gather up his writing and exit the apartment.)

WOMAN. (*Off.*) You never bone me.

MANNY. Button your lip.

SHELLY. Maybe he would if you were at home.

MANNY. You stay out of this lady or I'll slap you into the middle of next week.

WOMAN. (*Off.*) You said you wanted to bone her, didn't you?

MANNY. Like hell I did.

WOMAN. (*Off.*) No, I'm sorry, you said you wanted to poke her.

SHELLY. Poke *me*?

MANNY. I didn't say I wanted to, I said I wouldn't mind.

SHELLY. (*Utterly disgusted.*) What a sick thought.

(*Pause.*)

MANNY. I'm gonna break your face, little buddy. Hey, get back here.

(*MANNY grabs STEVE, bringing him back into the apartment.*)

MANNY. You're gonna deal with this. Are you boning my wife?
SHELLY. Leave him alone.
MANNY. I'm warning you, mousy ...
WOMAN. (*Coming out of the bathroom.*) Manny, stop it! He didn't do anything to me.
SHELLY. He didn't?
MANNY. Then what the hell are you doing here at two o'clock a.m. in the morning?
WOMAN. I wanted him to but he wouldn't.
SHELLY. He wouldn't?
MANNY. What's the matter, my wife's not good enough for ya? Too fat for ya or something?
STEVE. Look, I ... I was, I wanted to write. That's all I wanted to do.
SHELLY. Tell me about it.
MANNY. Then why ain't you writing?
STEVE. Because I'm unscrewing birdfeeders.

MANNY. What were you doing in here with the feeder?

STEVE. Look, it isn't just the feeder. I'm talking about redheads and gopher patches ...

WOMAN. It's my feeder.

SHELLY. I said I didn't care about the ...

MANNY. You don't even like the thing.

STEVE. And we're discussing fantasy fun kits. You got your cuffs, jellies, plugs; oh and of course, the pulsating pal.

WOMAN. That's because you're never home to enjoy it with me.

SHELLY. Steven! You told them about that?

STEVE. ... No, Shelly ... I didn't tell anybody anything. I'm too busy listening to tales of Colorado and Robert buying you drinks and kids teasing each other about who's Manny and who's not.

MANNY. Hey, I—I made that up.

WOMAN. Manny, I heard. Why didn't you tell me?

MANNY. I made it up.

WOMAN. Manny.

STEVE. Look folks, can we take this somewhere else?

MANNY. In a minute, little buddy.

STEVE. What do you people want from me?

SHELLY. I still want you, Steven.

STEVE. No, Shelly, you don't want me, you want me the way you wish I were.

SHELLY. I want a normal relationship, is that too much to ask?

STEVE. You tell me. I'm giving you everything I can.

SHELLY. I need more.

STEVE. I know. I'm sorry.

SHELLY. So am I. *(Starts to leave.)*

WOMAN. No! He didn't do anything.

STEVE. Look, she knows that.

WOMAN. But you gotta tell her.

STEVE. What am I supposed to tell her?! That I'm trying to figure out if I can be what I want to be? And the possibility that I just might not have what it takes scares the hell out of me and I know if I can't have it, I can't have her?

MANNY. Yeah, tell her that.

SHELLY. It doesn't make any sense.

WOMAN. Yeah, it does. Doesn't it, Manny?

STEVE. It isn't that simple. Is it, Shelly?

SHELLY. Look, Steven, I know you said it would be all the time, I just didn't know it would be all the time.

STEVE. I know. Look, do you want to be them?

MANNY. What the hell is that supposed to mean?

STEVE. Figure it out, Einstein.

SHELLY. Hey, Steven, don't ...

MANNY. You can't talk to me that way, I'm the manager!

STEVE. No, I'm the fucking manager!!!

SHELLY. You don't have to be mean.

STEVE. Why? Being nice sure isn't getting me anywhere.

MANNY. Hey, settle down pal.

STEVE. Don't tell me to settle down. I'm the manager remember?

MANNY. Fine, fine. You're the manager.

STEVE. Let me ask you something, Manny. Do you want to be you?

MANNY. What's that got to do with anything?

STEVE. Manny, you're hiding from each other. You're hiding!

MANNY. You think you're the only guy that ever wanted to make something out of his life?

STEVE. No.

WOMAN. Well you're not. Okay?

STEVE. Okay.

MANNY. You wanted to bone this guy?

WOMAN. I wanted something, I don't know if it was that, but something.

MANNY. Why didn't you get it from me?

WOMAN. Cuz you're never home.

MANNY. That's 'cuz whenever I'm home you're always bitching 'cuz I'm never home.

(WOMAN and MANNY break apart.)

STEVE. You see that? Look, Shelly, we get rid of the woman in the bathroom and gopher patches and attractive asses and you still have a problem with how much time I spend with my writing.

SHELLY. You've said enough.

STEVE. No, I haven't. I realize that now. I've said just enough to keep you here. But you need more.

(Pause.)

SHELLY. I'm sorry.

STEVE. So am I, baby.

(STEVE and SHELLY hug.)

SHELLY. Hey, I didn't mean to call you ...

WOMAN. I didn't mean to moo at you ... either ...

SHELLY. Hey, it's okay. *(Goes to the door.)* Hope to see you on the Best Seller list.

(SHE exits. STEVE watches after her a moment. Then turns and sees MANNY and the WOMAN watching him and standing off from each other. After a moment, STEVE sits in the arm chair and looks at them, raises his arms as if to say "What?")

WOMAN. Manny, are we gonna be them?

(Pause.)

STEVE. Take her home, Manny.

MANNY. Wanna?

(MANNY looks at the Woman. SHE nods, then goes, gets the feeder and waits. MANNY goes to the table and picks up his money.)

MANNY. Hey, thanks for not boning my wife. *(MANNY starts out, sees the bottle of wine, picks it up, looks at the Woman, then crosses back to Steve.)* Mind?

(STEVE takes the bottle of wine. Looks at it, then at the Woman, then hands the bottle back to MANNY.)

STEVE. Not at all.

(MANNY slaps his money back on the table. HE and the WOMAN start out. The WOMAN turns back and looks at Steve.)

WOMAN. Toodle loo.
STEVE. Toodle loo.

(MANNY and the WOMAN exit. STEVE looks at his typewriter. After a moment, HE gets up, puts on some MUSIC, goes back to his typewriter and begins to type.
FADE OUT.)

END OF PLAY

DIRECTOR'S NOTES

Though the play is set in Las Cruces, New Mexico I don't feel this is an essential geographic location. What is important is that it is set in a small college town. If you wish to place it in a college town near you, feel free. My concern lies in a tendency I have noticed in the stereotypical depiction of small Southwestern towns and of the dress and speech of the people, i.e. big belt buckles, wacky hats and boots, thick drawls, etc. Which brings me to a second more important point: All people and events in this play are real. Any similarity to situation comedies, living or dead, is purely coincidental and the tendency to treat the play as such should be avoided.

PROPERTY LIST

Typewriter
Papers (typewritten, notes and scratch)
Pens, pencils, Waste basket
Telephone
Stereo/Cassette deck, cassettes
Coffee pot
Coffee cup(s)
Hummingbird feeder
Matches
Bottle of wine
Beers
Fingernail clippers
Ashtray
Wallet with money

SET PIECES

Table
Chairs
Bed
Wall heater
Kitchen sink
Tapestry (above bed)
Oven
Front door
Bathroom door
Window (w/curtains)

SOUND

Toilet flushing
Car peeling in/out (optional)
Rock & Roll (on stereo)

NEW COMEDIES FROM
SAMUEL FRENCH, INC.

MAIDS OF HONOR. (Little Theatre.) Comedy. Joan Casademont. 3m., 4f. Comb Int./Ext. Elizabeth McGovern, Laila Robins and Kyra Sedgwick starred in this warm, wacky comedy at Off-Broadway's famed WPA Theatre. Monica Bowlin, a local TV talk-show host, is getting married. Her two sisters, Isabelle and Annie, are intent on talking her out of it. It seems that Mr. Wonderful, the groom-to-be, is about to be indicted for insider trading, a little secret he has failed to share with his fiancee, Monica. She has a secret she has kept herself, too—she's pregnant, possibly not by her groom-to-be! All this is uncovered by delightfully kookie Isabelle, who aspires to be an investigative reporter. She'd also like to get Monica to realize that she is marrying the wrong man, for the wrong reason. She should be marrying ex-boyfriend Roger Dowling, who has come back to return a diary Monica left behind. And sister Annie should be marrying the caterer for the wedding, old flame Harry Hobson—but for some reason she can't relax enough to see how perfect he is for her. The reason for all three Bowlin women's difficulties with men, the reason why they have always made the wrong choice and failed to see the right one, is that they are the adult children of an alcoholic father and an abused mother, both now passed away, and they cannot allow themselves to love because they themselves feel unlovable. Sound gloomy and depressing? No, indeed. This delightful, wise and warm-hearted new play is loaded with laughs. We would also like to point out to all you actors that the play is also loaded with excellent monologues, at least one of which was recently included in an anthology of monologues from the best new plays.)   **(#14961)**

GROTESQUE LOVESONGS. (Little Theatre.) Comedy. Don Nigro. (Author of *The Curate Shakespeare As You Like It, Seascape with Sharks and Dancer* and other plays). This quirky new comedy about a family in Terre Haute, Indiana, enchanted audiences at NYC's famed WPA Theatre. Two brothers, Pete and John, live with their parents in a big old house with an attached greenhouse. The father, Dan, has a horticulture business. A pretty young woman named Romy is more or less engaged to marry younger brother Johnny as the play begins, and their prospects look quite rosy, for Johnny has just inherited a ton of money from recently-deceased family friend, Mr. Agajanian. Why, wonders Pete, has Agajanian left his entire estate to Johnny? He starts to persistently ask this question to his mother, Louise. Eventually, Louise does admit that, in fact, Mr. Agajanian was Johnny's father. This news stuns Johnny; but he's not *really* staggered until he goes down to the greenhouse and finds Pete and Romy making love. Pete, it seems, has always desperately wanted Romy; but when she chose Johnny instead he married a woman in the circus who turned out to be a con artist, taking him for everything he had and then disappearing. It seems everyone but Johnny is haunted by a traumatic past experience: Louise by her affair with Agajanian; Dan by the memory of his first true love, a Terre Haute whore; Pete by his failed marriage, and Romy by her *two* failed marriages. (One husband she left; the other was run over by a truckload of chickens [He loved cartoons so much, says Romy, that it was only fitting he should die like Wile E. Coyote.]). And, each character but Johnny knows what he wants. Louise and Dan want the contentment of their marriage; Romy wants to bake bread in a big old house—and she wants Pete, who finally admits that he wants her, too. And, finally, Johnny realizes what he wants. He does not want the money, or Agajanian's house. He wants to go to Nashville to make his own way as a singer of sad—yes, grotesque—love songs in the night. NOTE: this play is a treasure-trove of scene and monologue material.)   **(#9925)**

TWO NEW COMEDIES FROM
——— SAMUEL FRENCH, Inc.———

FAST GIRLS. **(Little Theatre). Comedy.** Diana Amsterdam. 2m., 3f. Int. Lucy Lewis is a contemporary, single woman in her thirties with what used to be called a "healthy sex life," much to the chagrin of her mother, who feels Lucy is too fast, too easy—and too single. Her best friend, on the other hand, neighbor Abigail McBride, is deeply envious of Lucy's ease with men. When Lucy wants to date a man she just calls him up, whereas Abigail sits home alone waiting for Ernest, who may not even know she exists, to call. The only time Abigail isn't by the phone is after Lucy has had a hot date, when she comes over to Lucy's apartment to hear the juicy details and get green with envy. Sometimes, though, Lucy doesn't want to talk about it, which drives Abigail *nuts* ("If you don't tell me about men I have no love life!"). Lucy's mother arrives to take the bull by the horns, so to speak, arriving with a challenge. Mom claims no man will marry Lucy (even were she to *want to* get married), because she's too easy. Lucy takes up the challenge, announcing that she is going to get stalwart ex-boyfriend Sidney ("we're just friends") Epstein to propose to her. Easier said than done. Sidney doesn't *want* a fast girl. Maybe dear old Mom is right, thinks Lucy. Maybe fast girls *can't* have it all. "Amsterdam makes us laugh, listen and think."—Daily Record. "Brilliantly comic moments."—The Monitor. "rapidly paced comedy with a load of laughs . . . a funny entertainment with some pause for reflection on today's [sexual] confusion."—Suburban News. "Takes a penetrating look at [contemporary sexual chaos]. Passion, celibacy, marriage, fidelity are just some of the subjects that Diana Amsterdam hilariously examines."—Tribune News. **(#8149)**

ADVICE FROM A CATERPILLAR. **(Little Theatre.) Comedy.** Douglas Carter Beane. 2m. 2f. 1 Unit set & 1 Int. Ally Sheedy and Dennis Christopher starred in the delightful off-Broadway production of this hip new comedy. Ms. Sheedy played Missy, an avant garde video artist who specializes in re-runs of her family's home videos, adding her own disparaging remarks. Needless to say, she is very alienated from the middle-class, family values she grew up with, which makes her very *au courant*, but strangely unhappy. She has a successful career and a satisfactory love-life with a businessman named Suit. Suit's married, but that doesn't stop him and Missy from carrying on. Something's missing, though—and Missy isn't sure what it is, until she meets Brat. He is a handsome young aspiring actor. Unfortunately, Brat is also the boyfriend of Missy's best friend. Sound familiar? It isn't—because Missy's best friend is a gay man named Spaz! Spaz has been urging Missy to find an unmarried boyfriend, but this is too much—too much for Spaz, too much for Suit and, possibly, too much for Missy. Does she *want* a serious relationship (ugh—how bourgeois!)? Can a bisexual unemployed actor actually be her Mr. Wonderful? "Very funny ... a delightful evening."—Town & Village. **(#3876)**